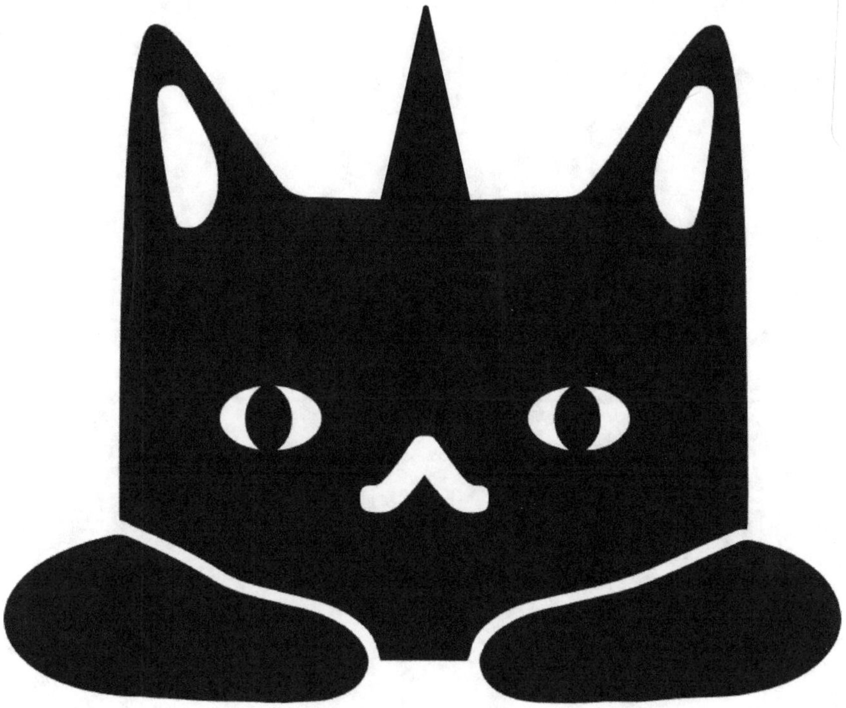

THIS BOOK BELONGS TO :

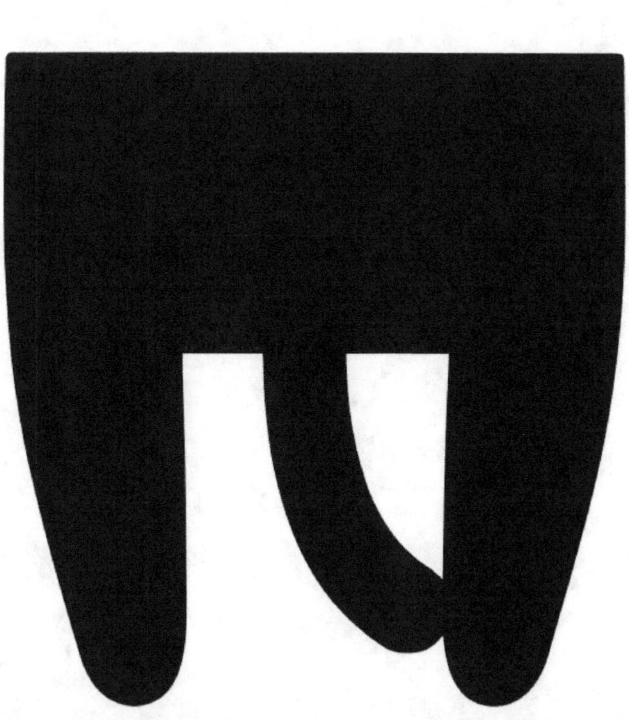

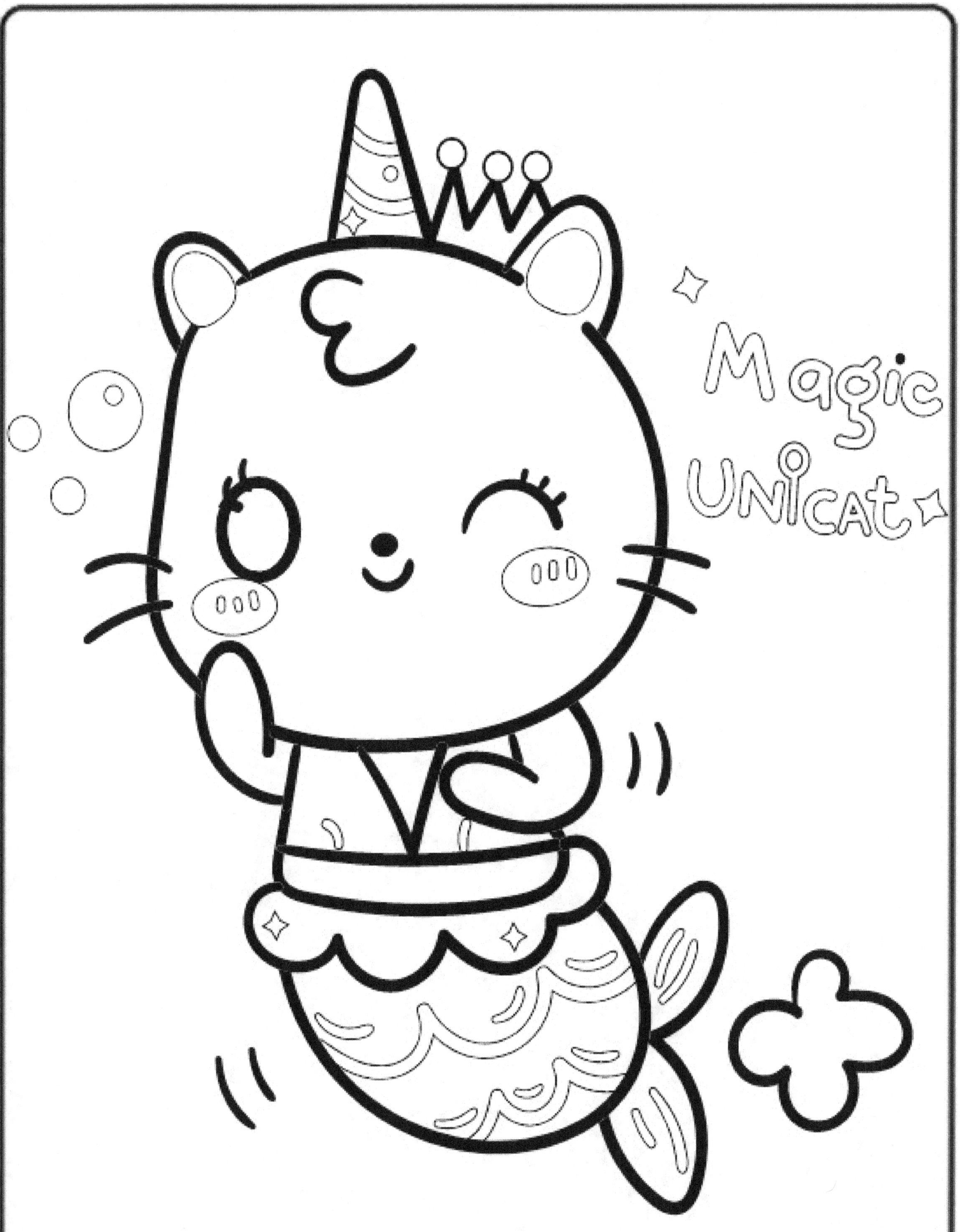
Magic
Unicat

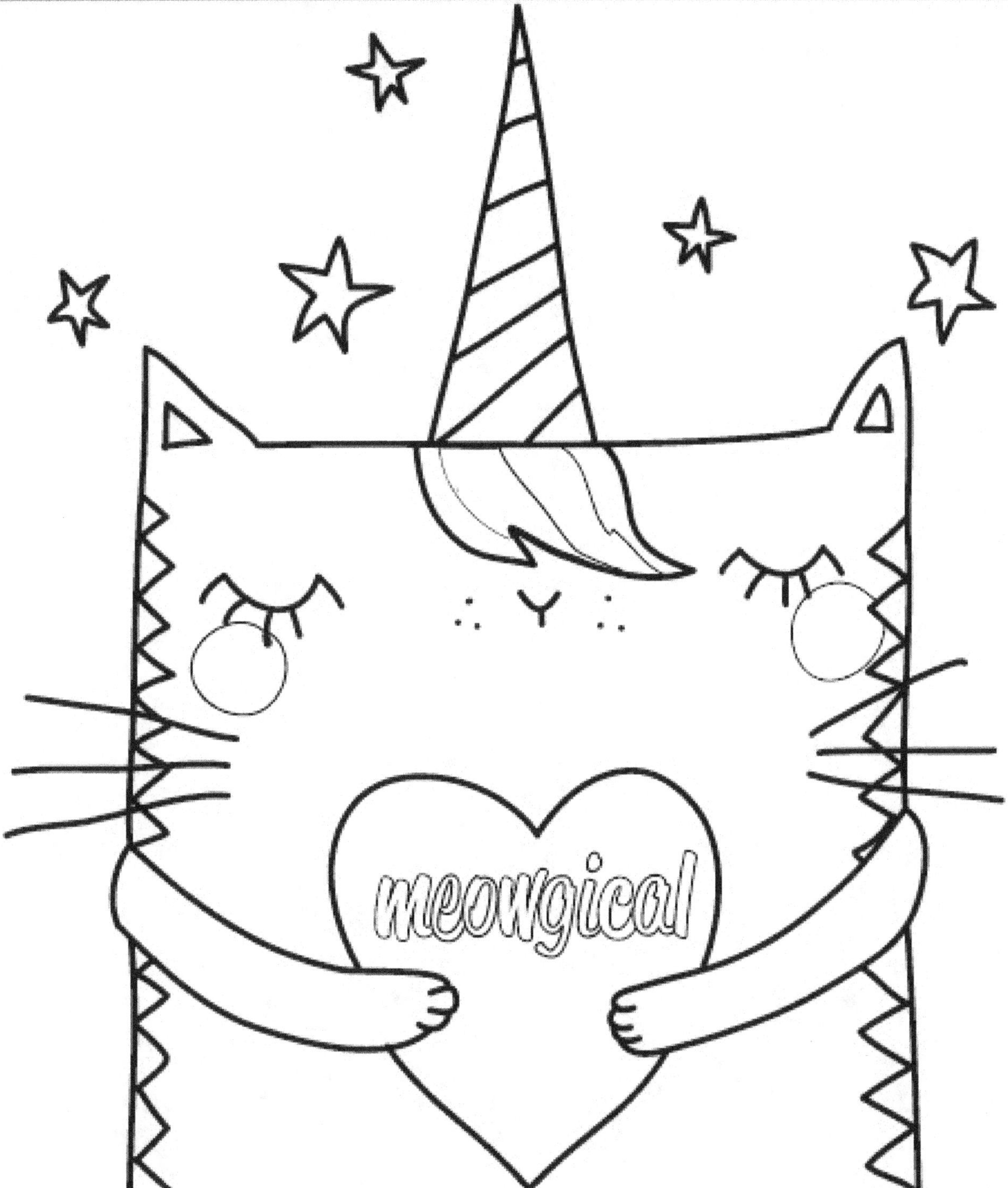
meowgical

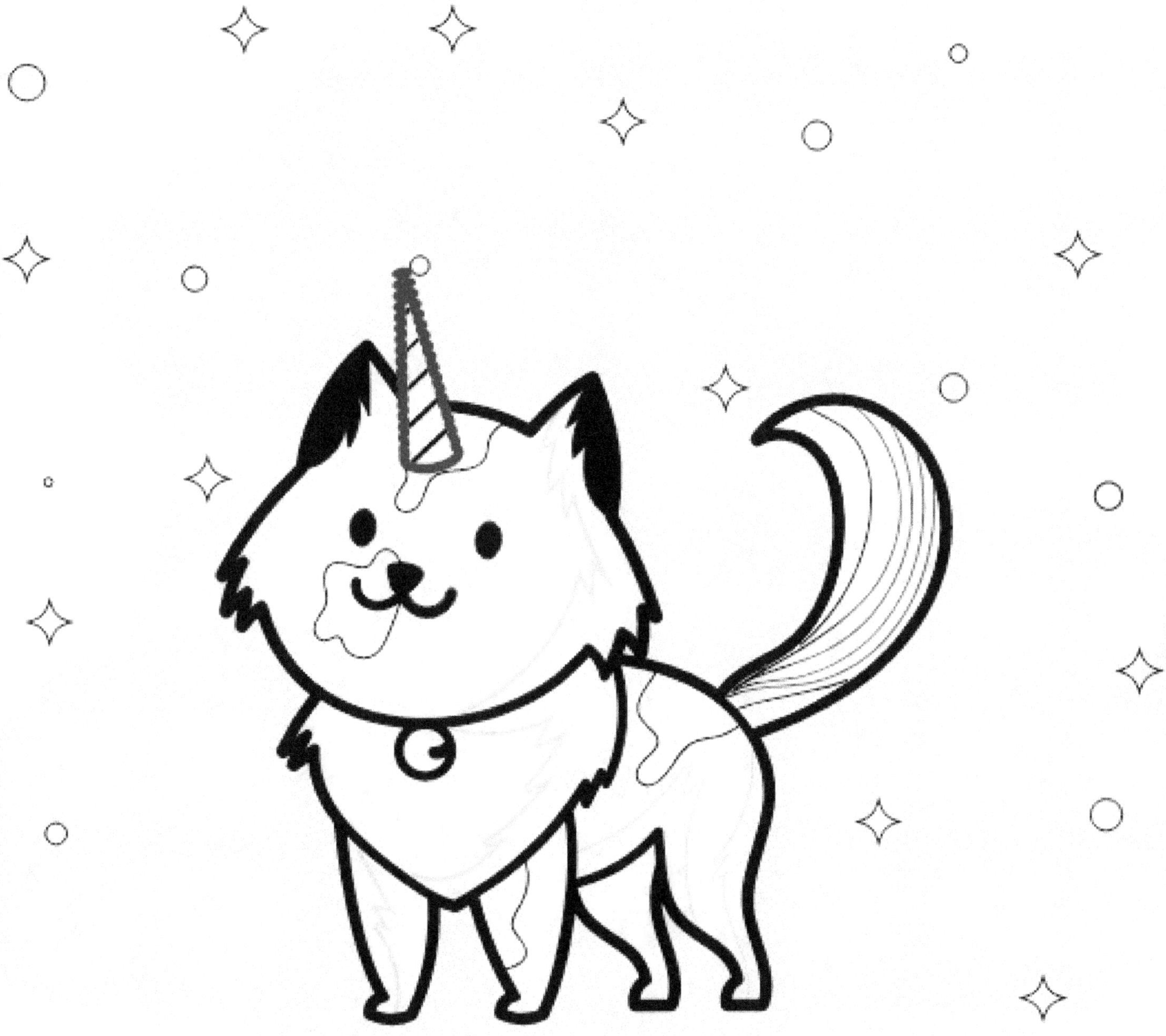

CATICORN

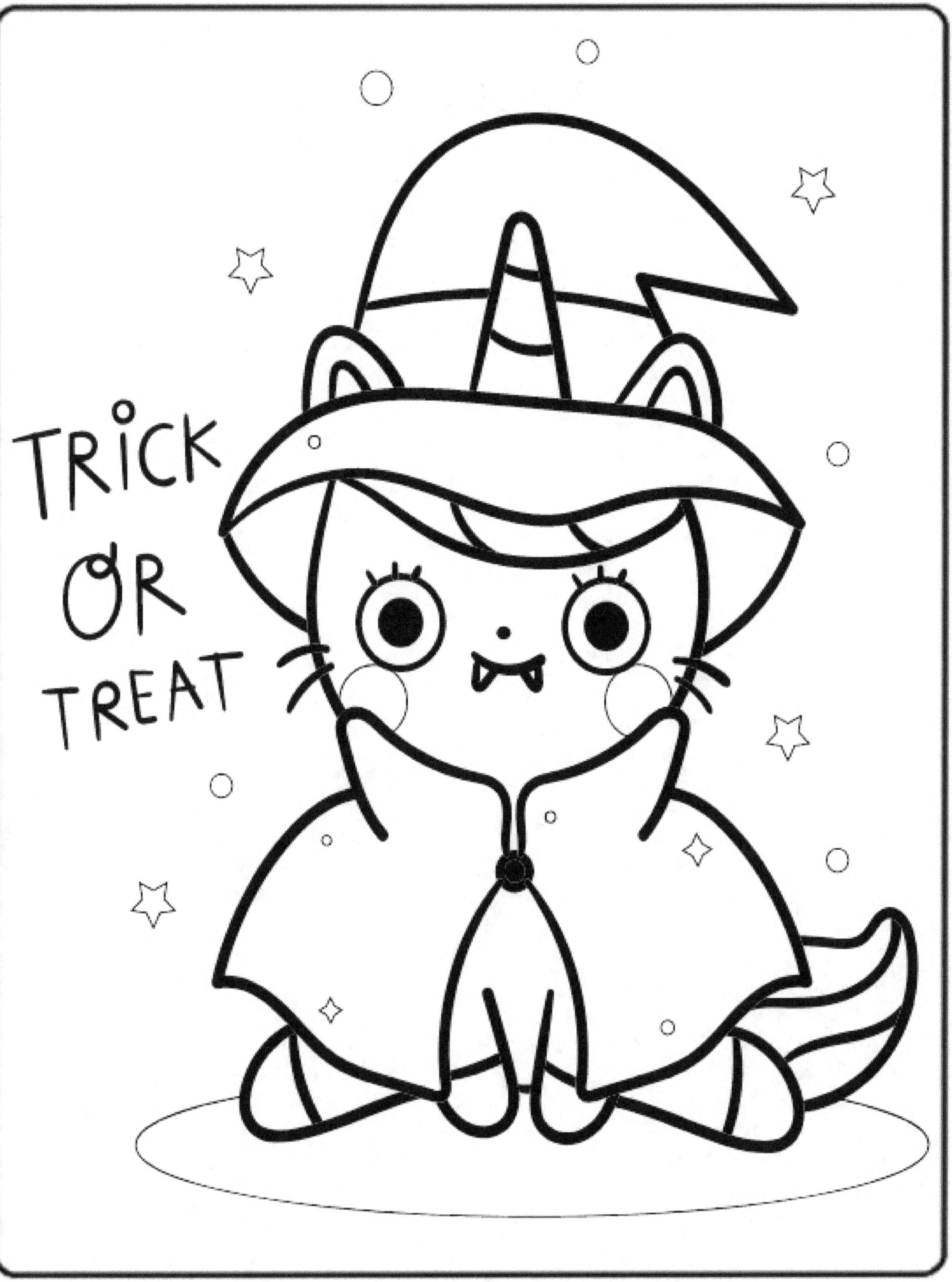
TRICK
OR
TREAT

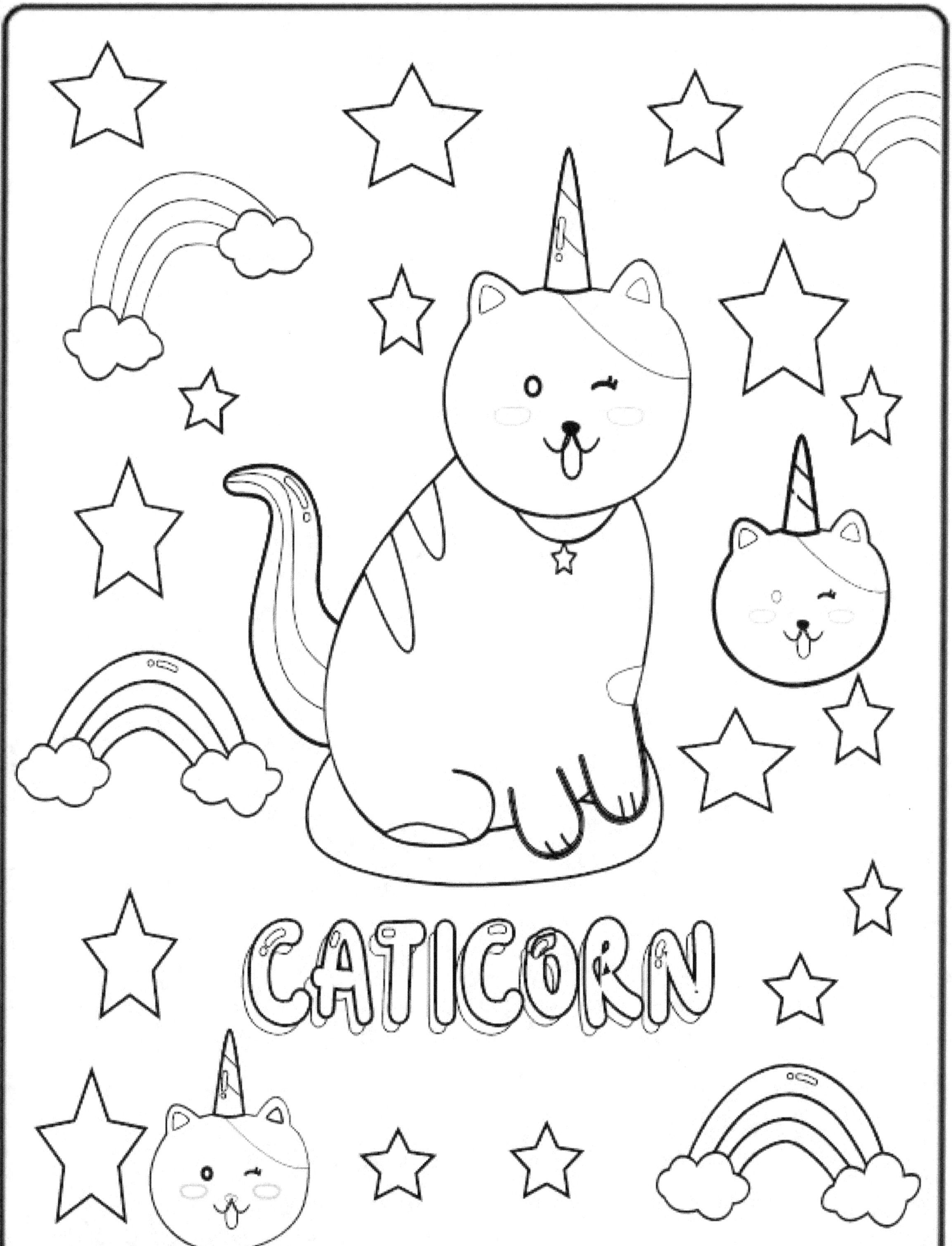
CATICORN

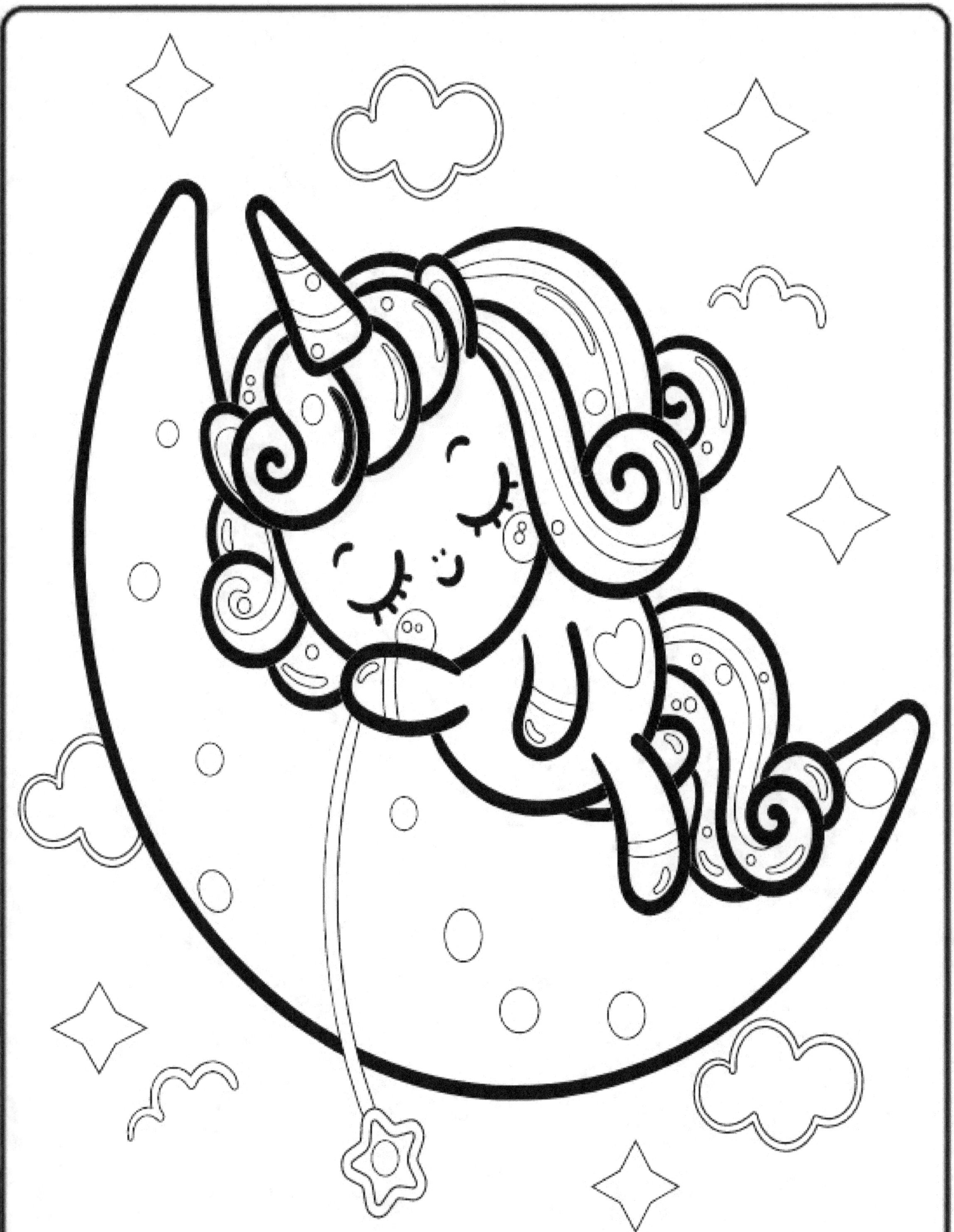

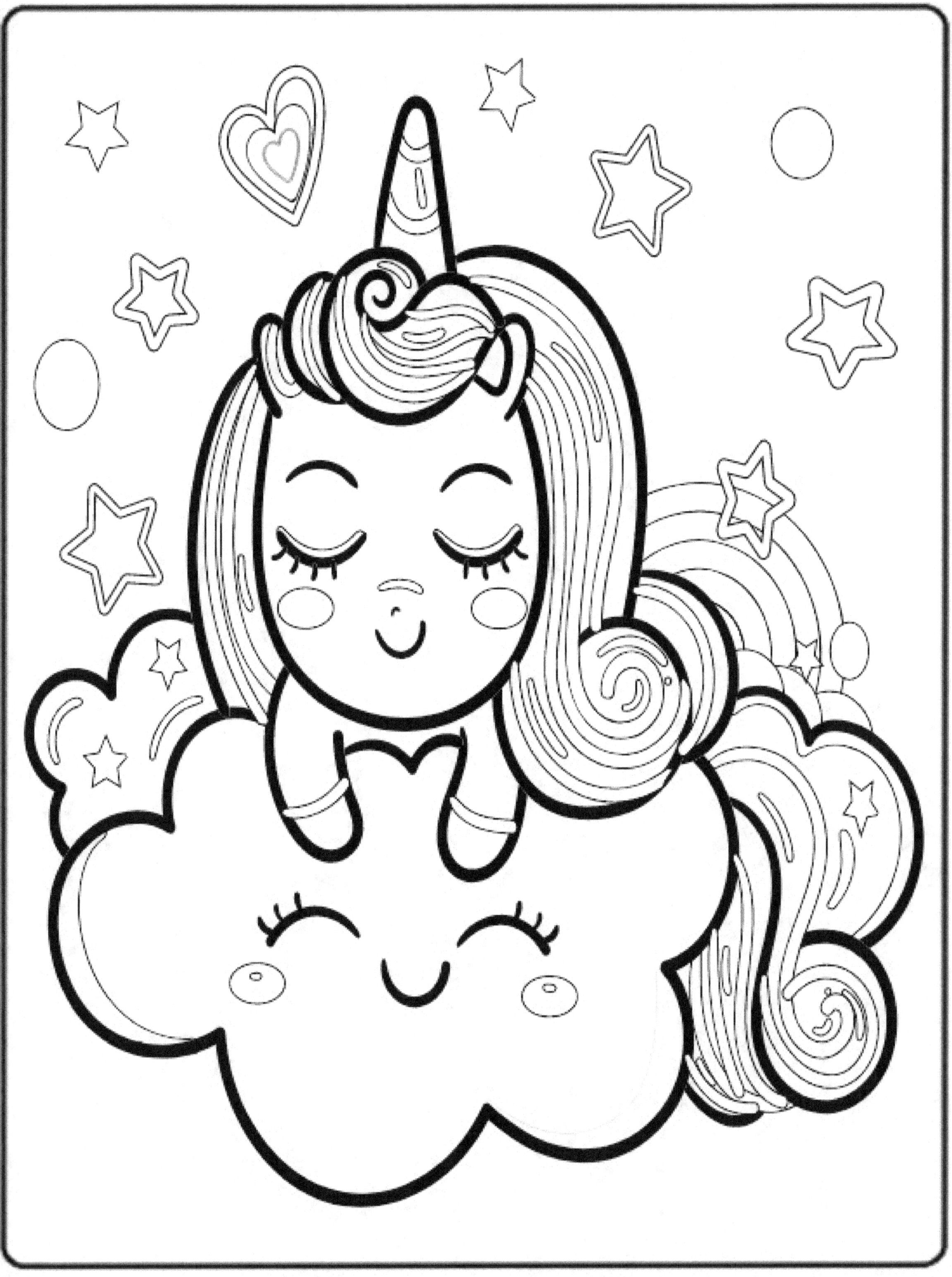

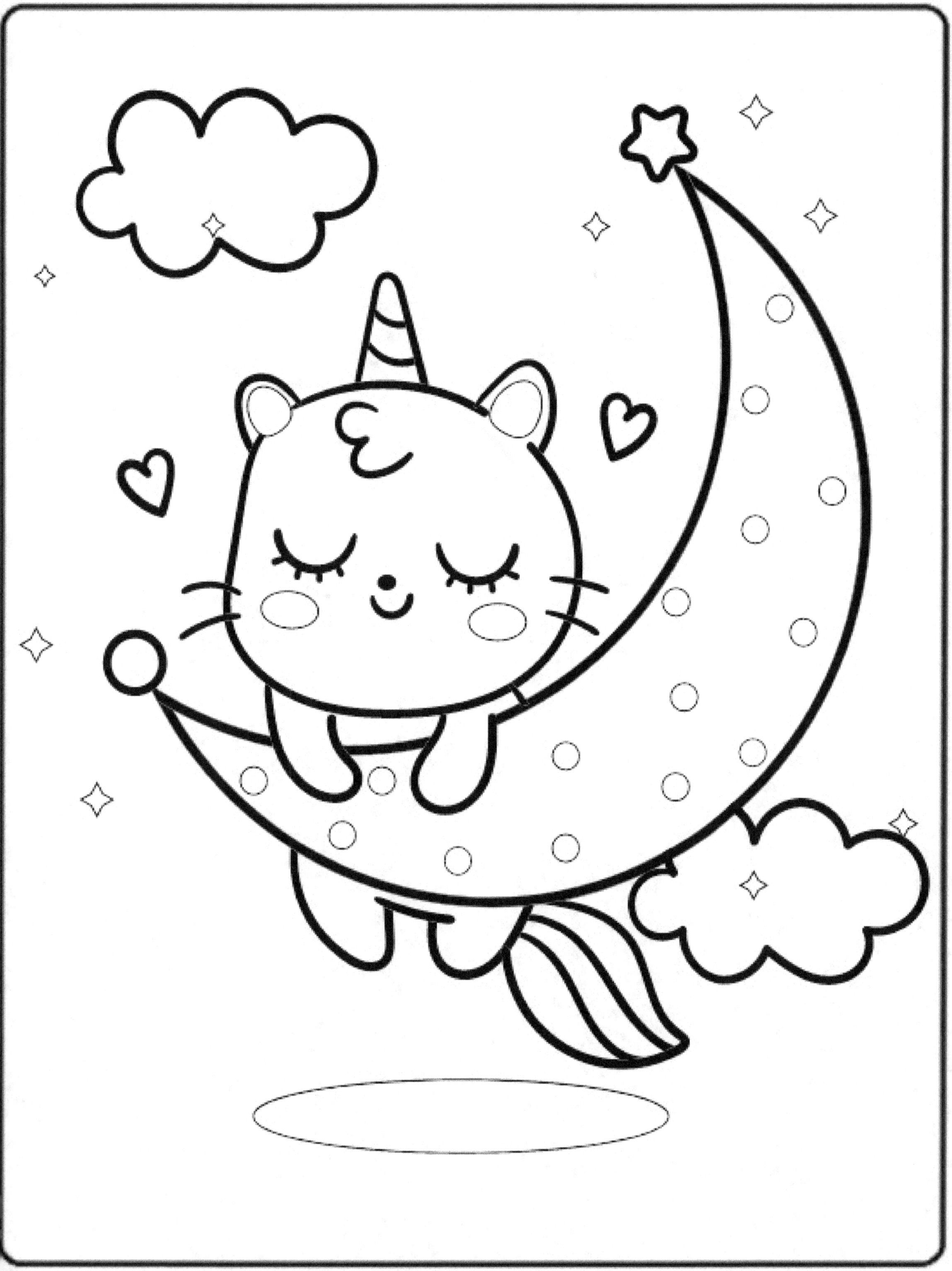

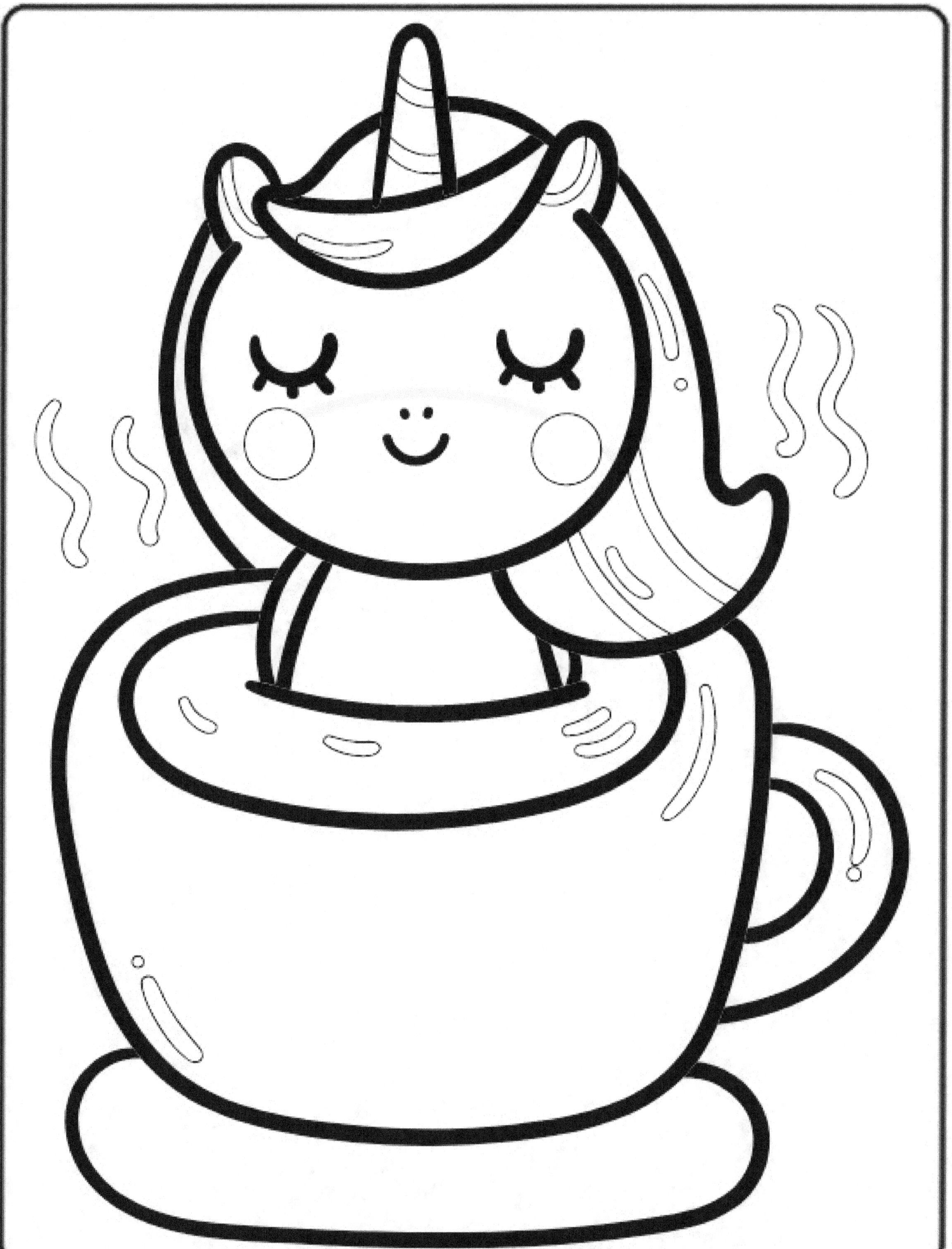

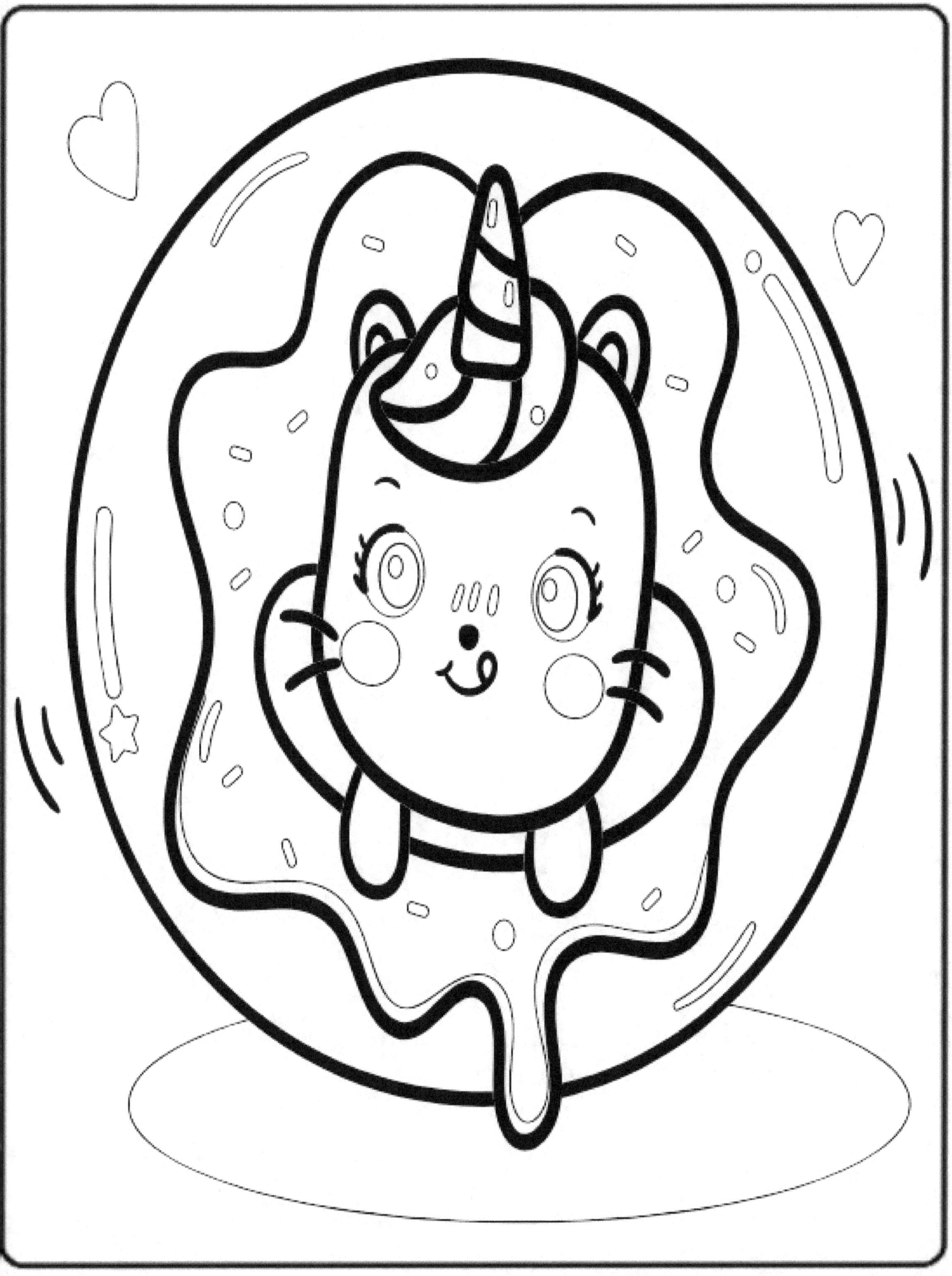

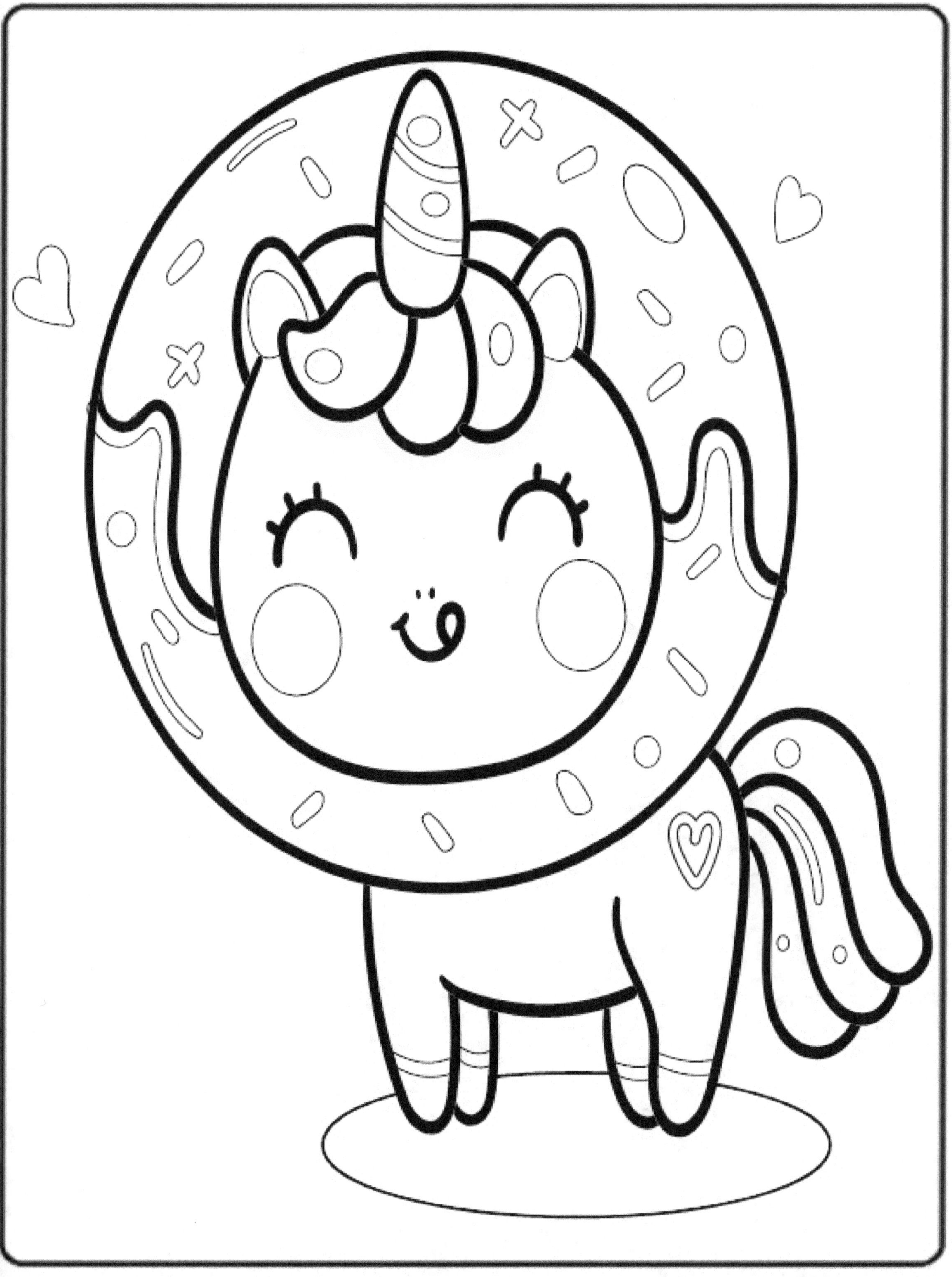

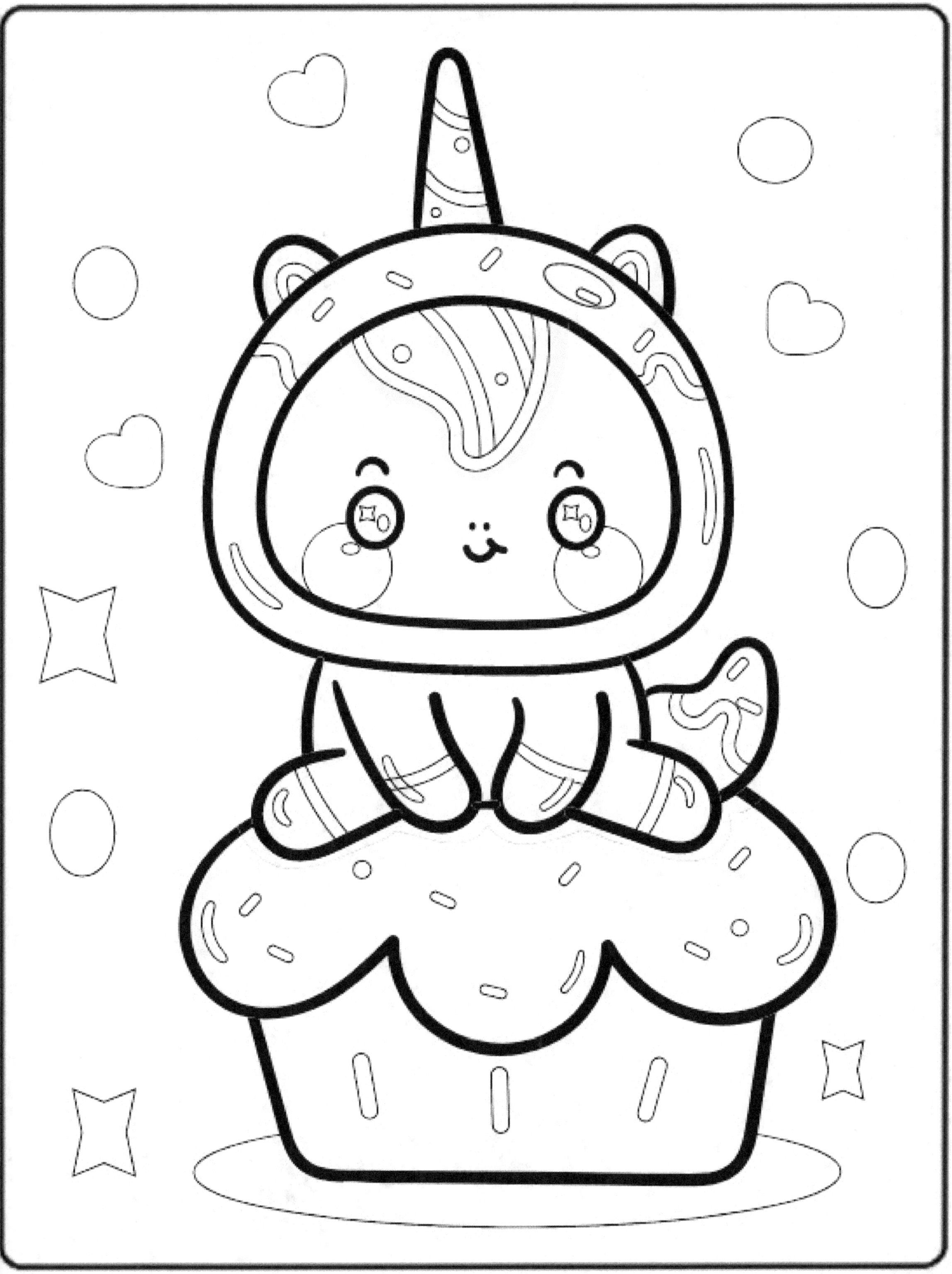

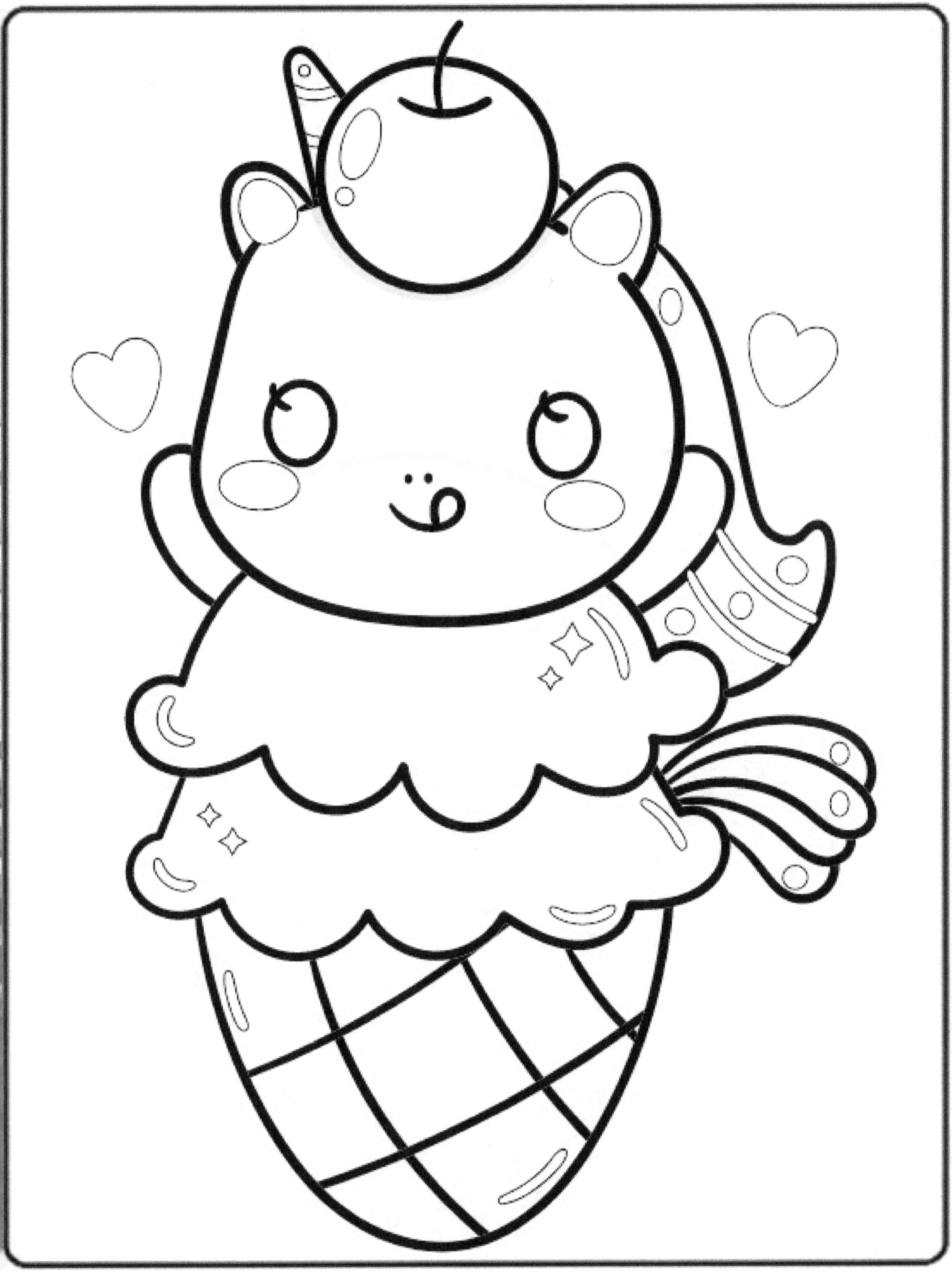

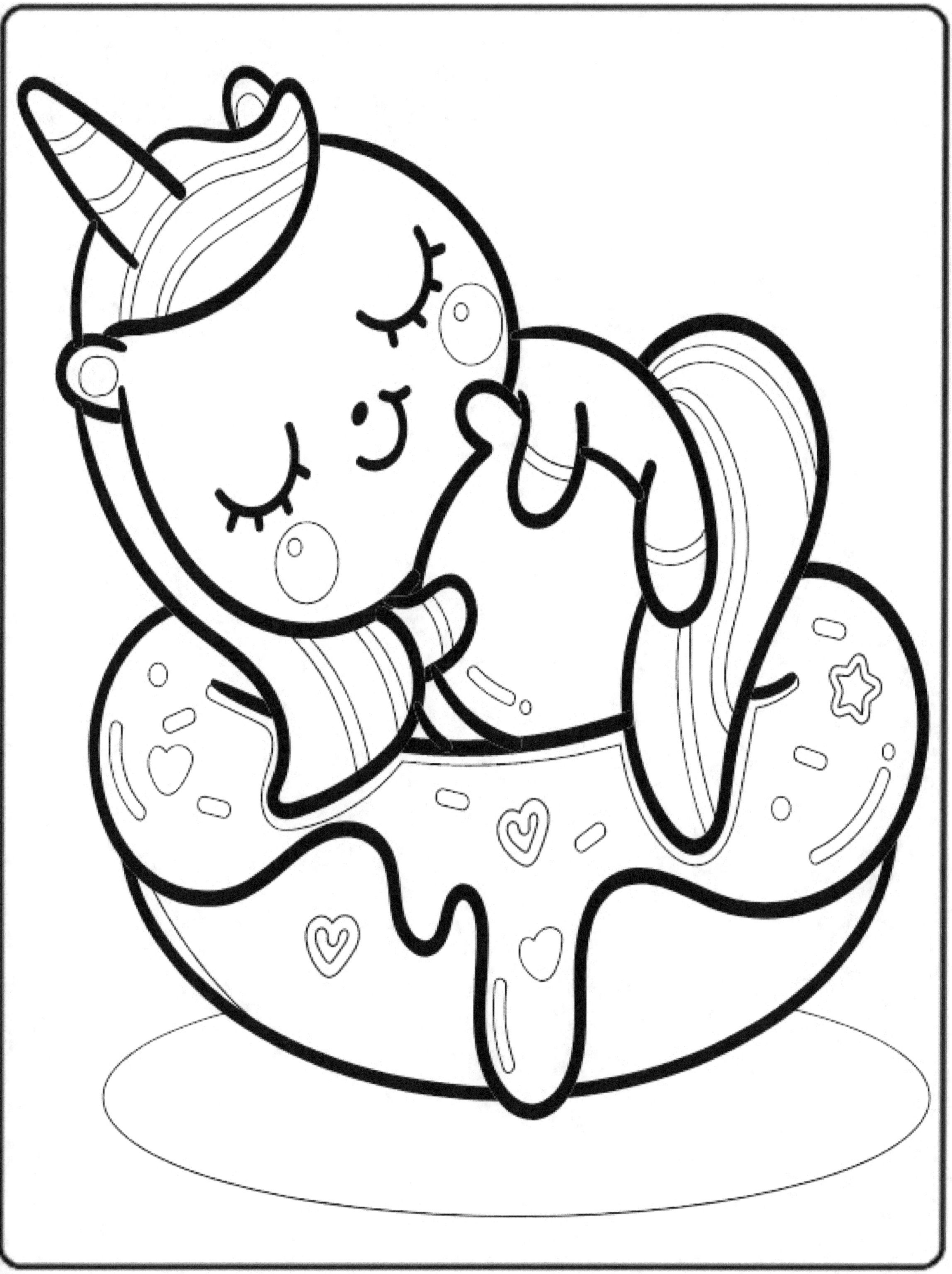

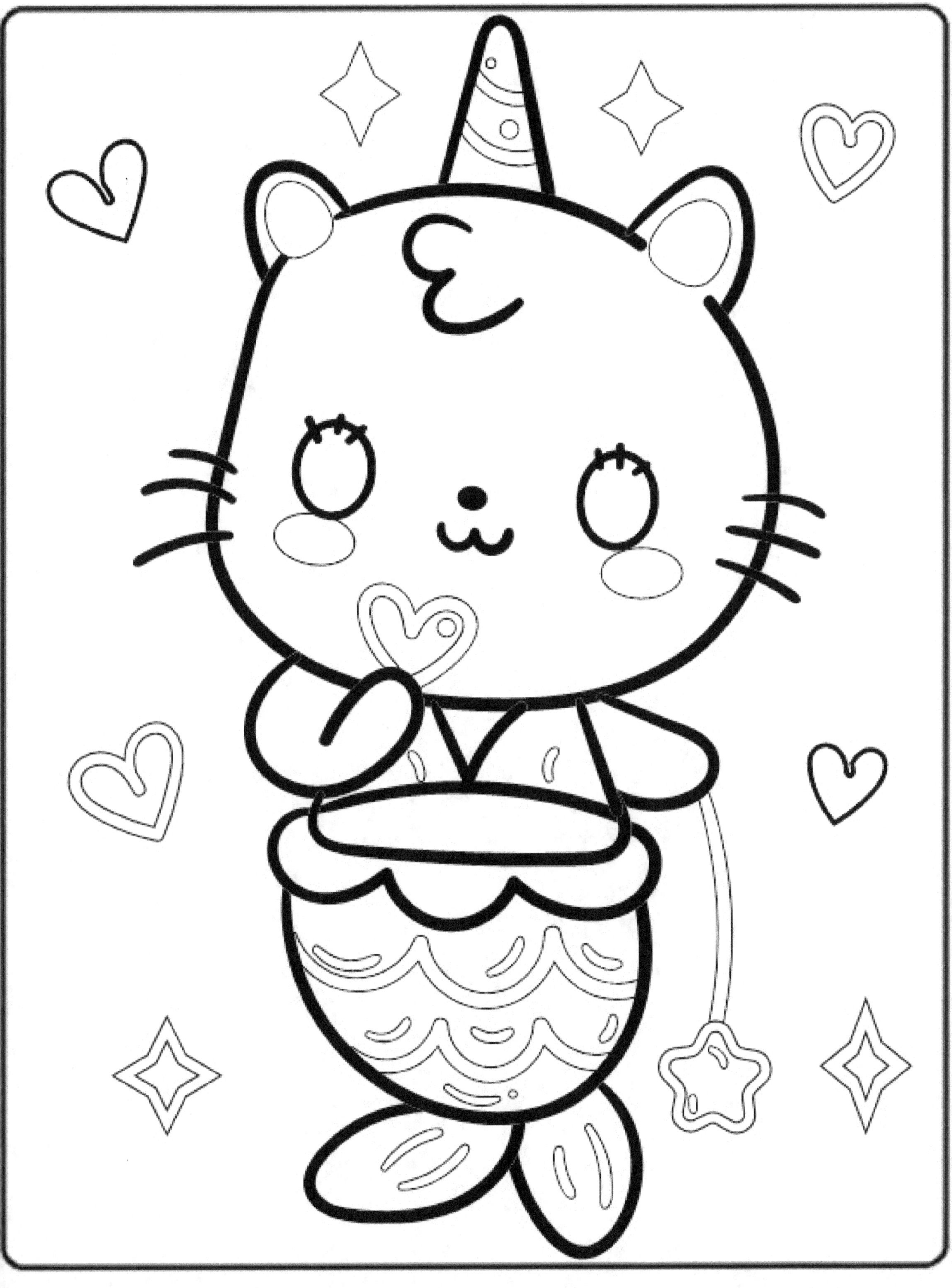

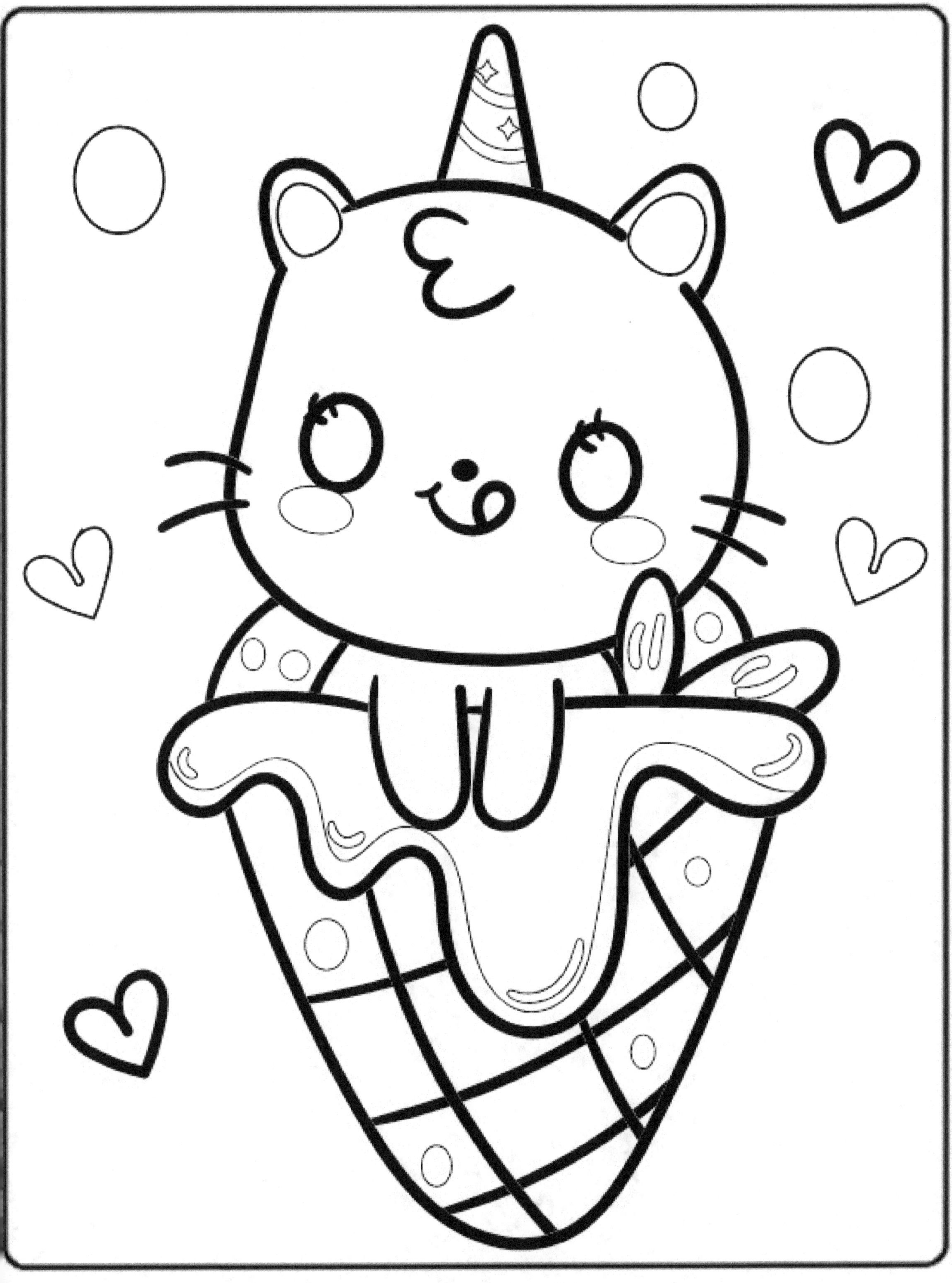

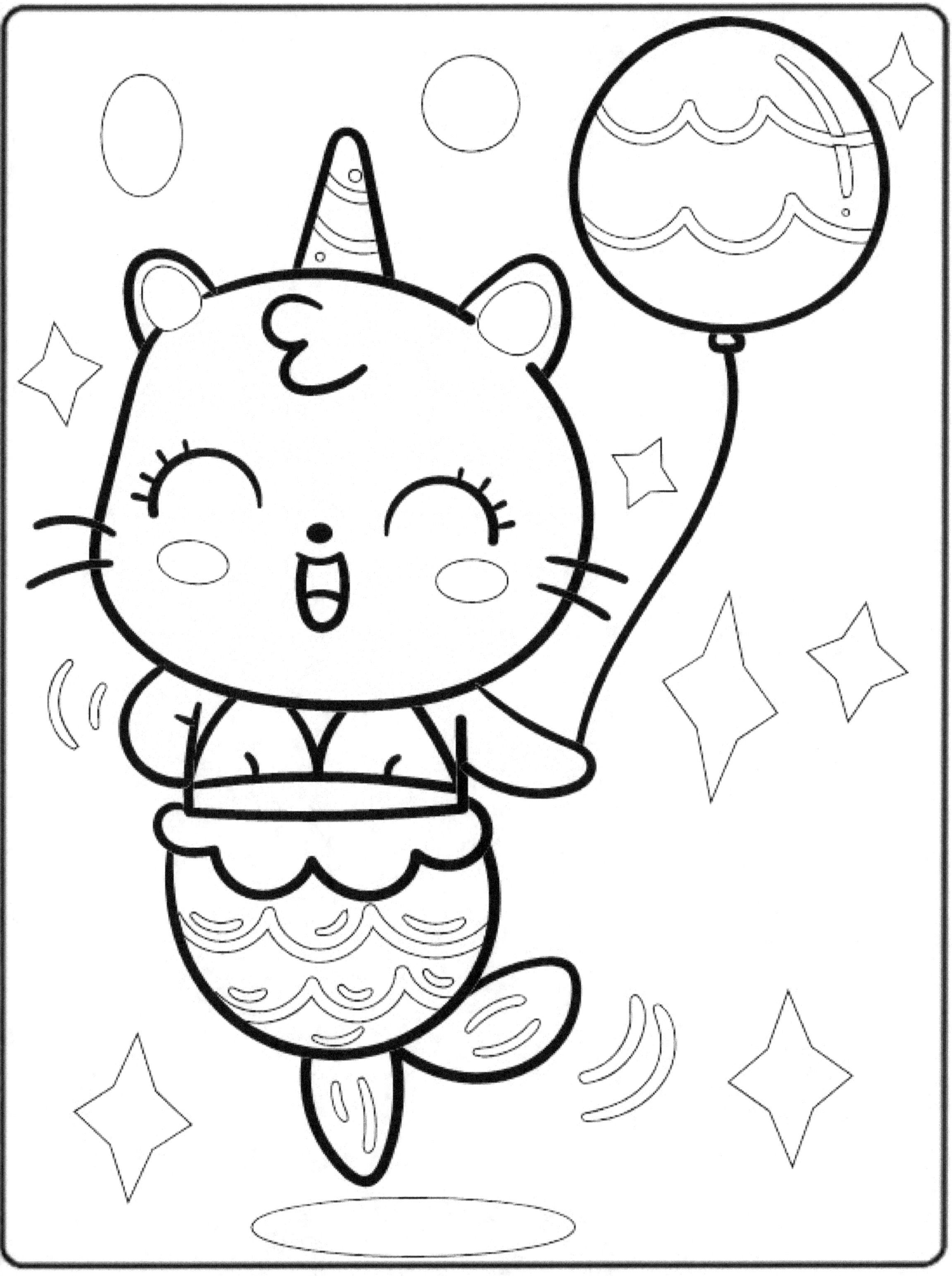

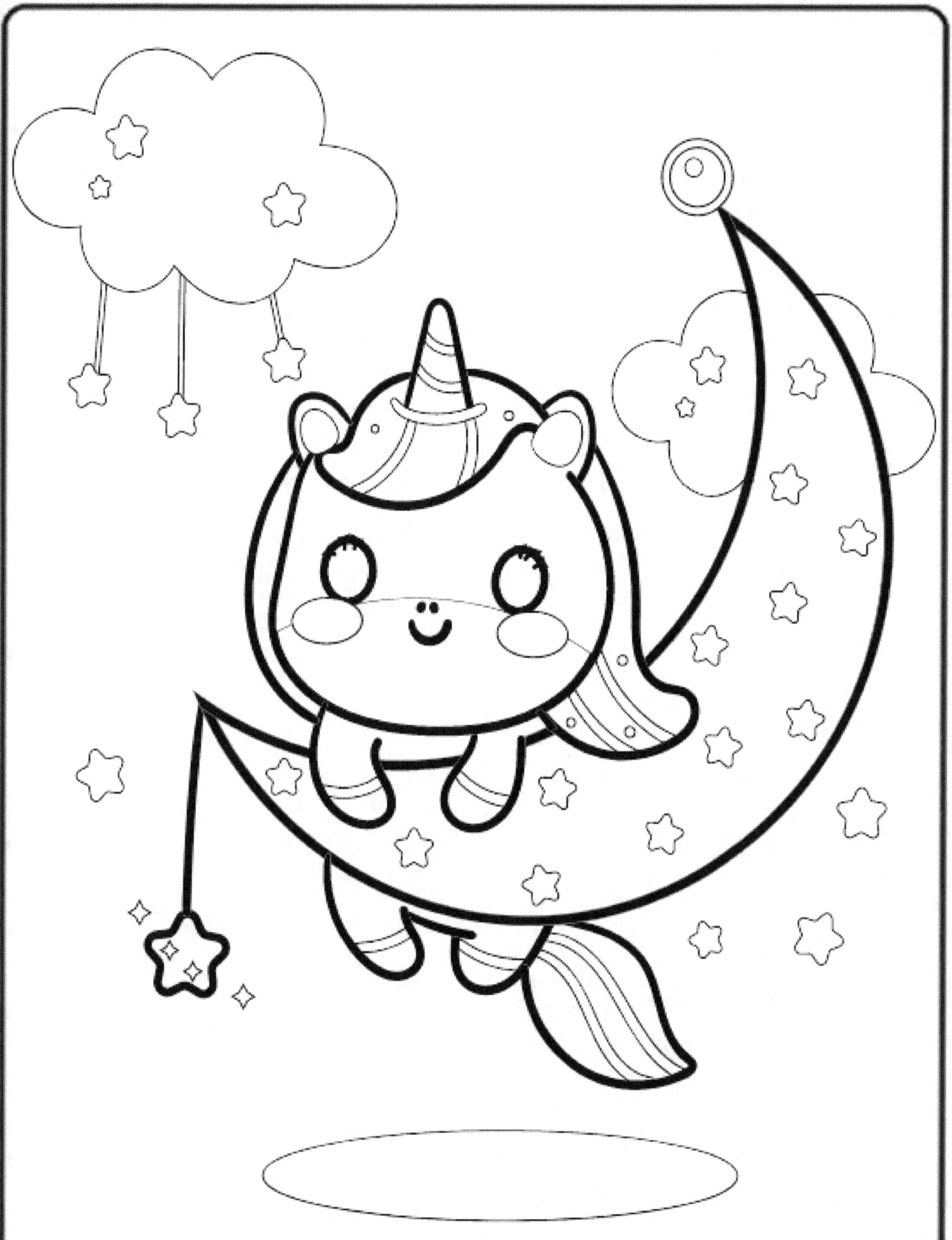

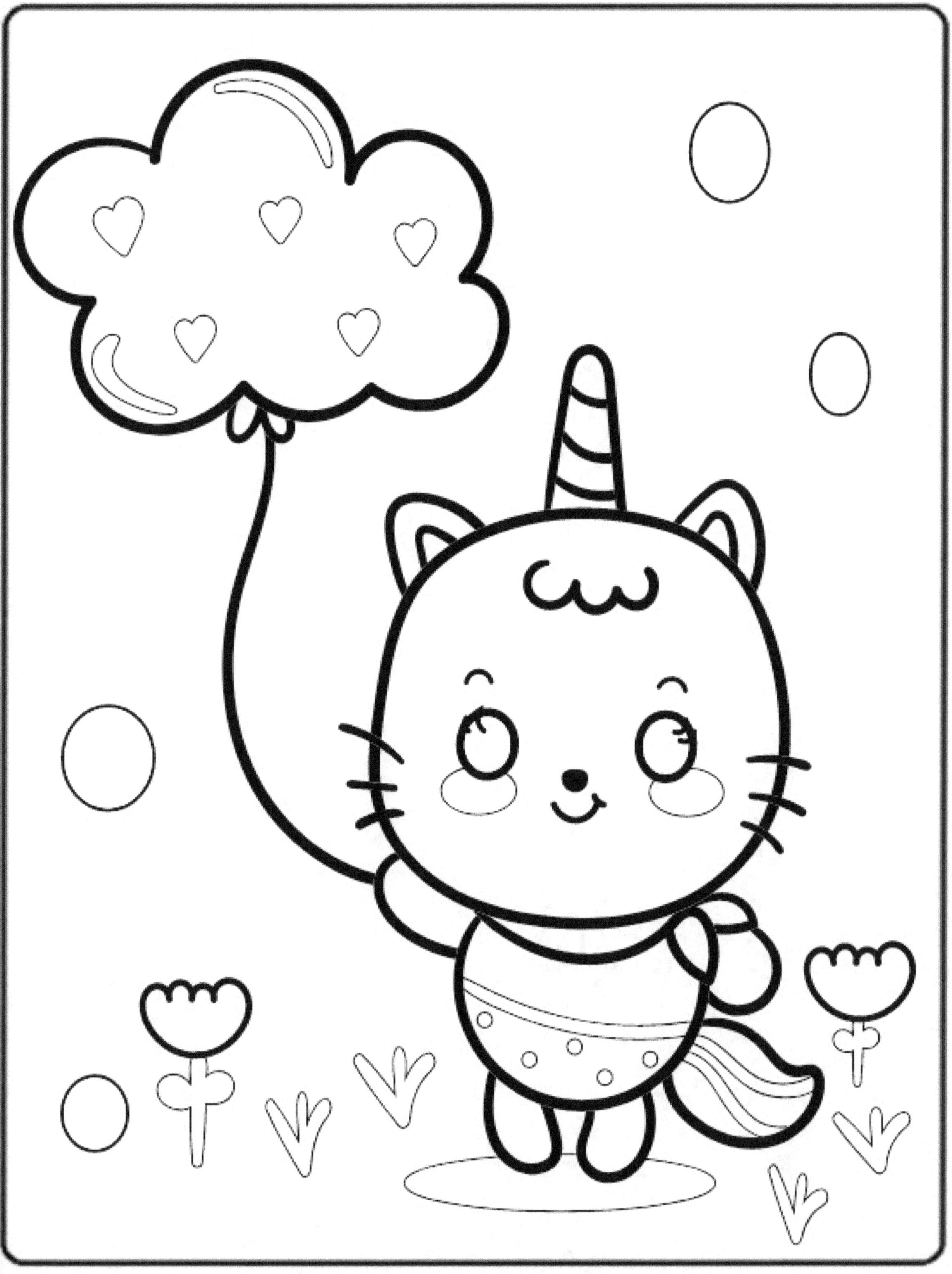

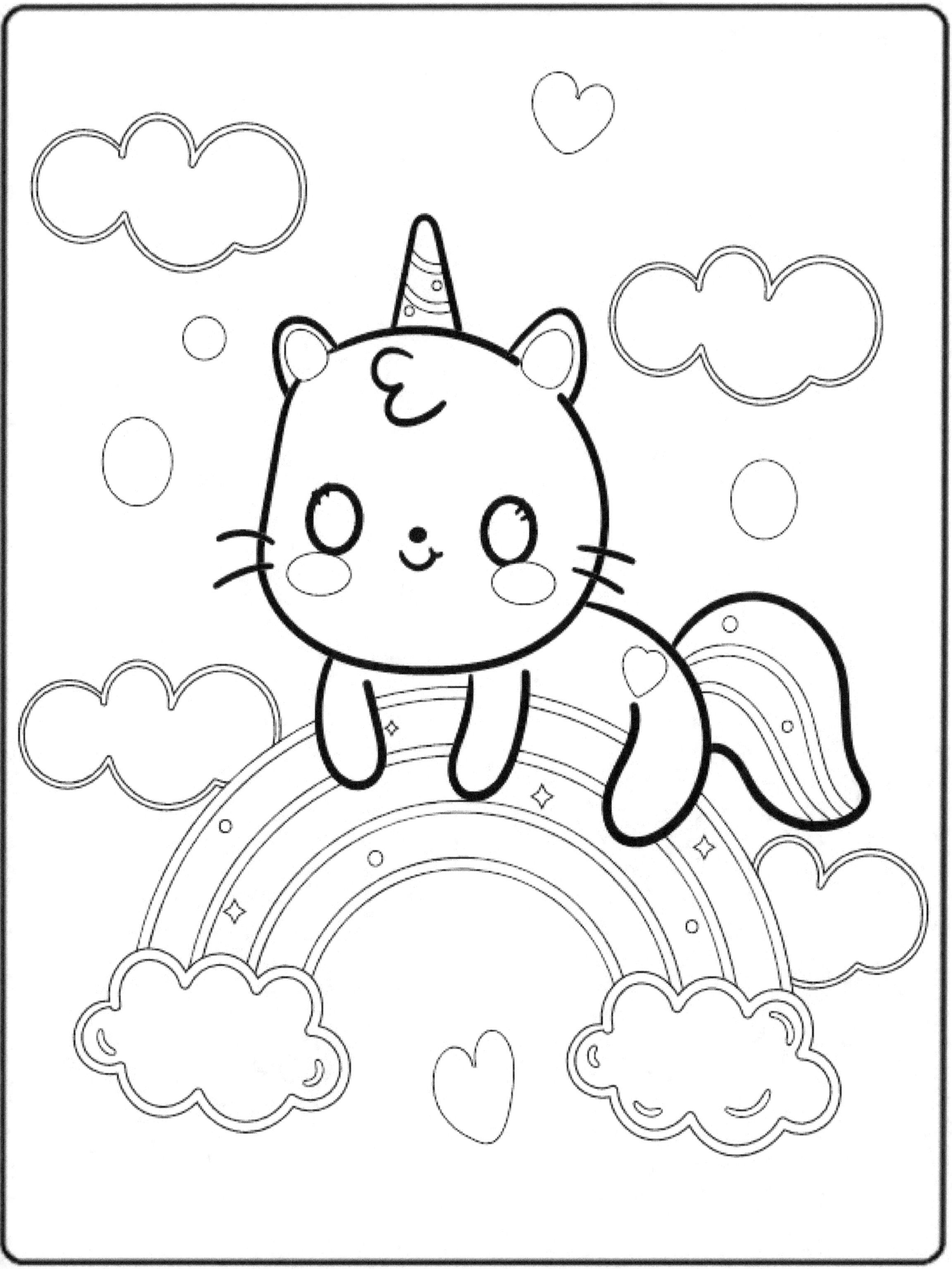

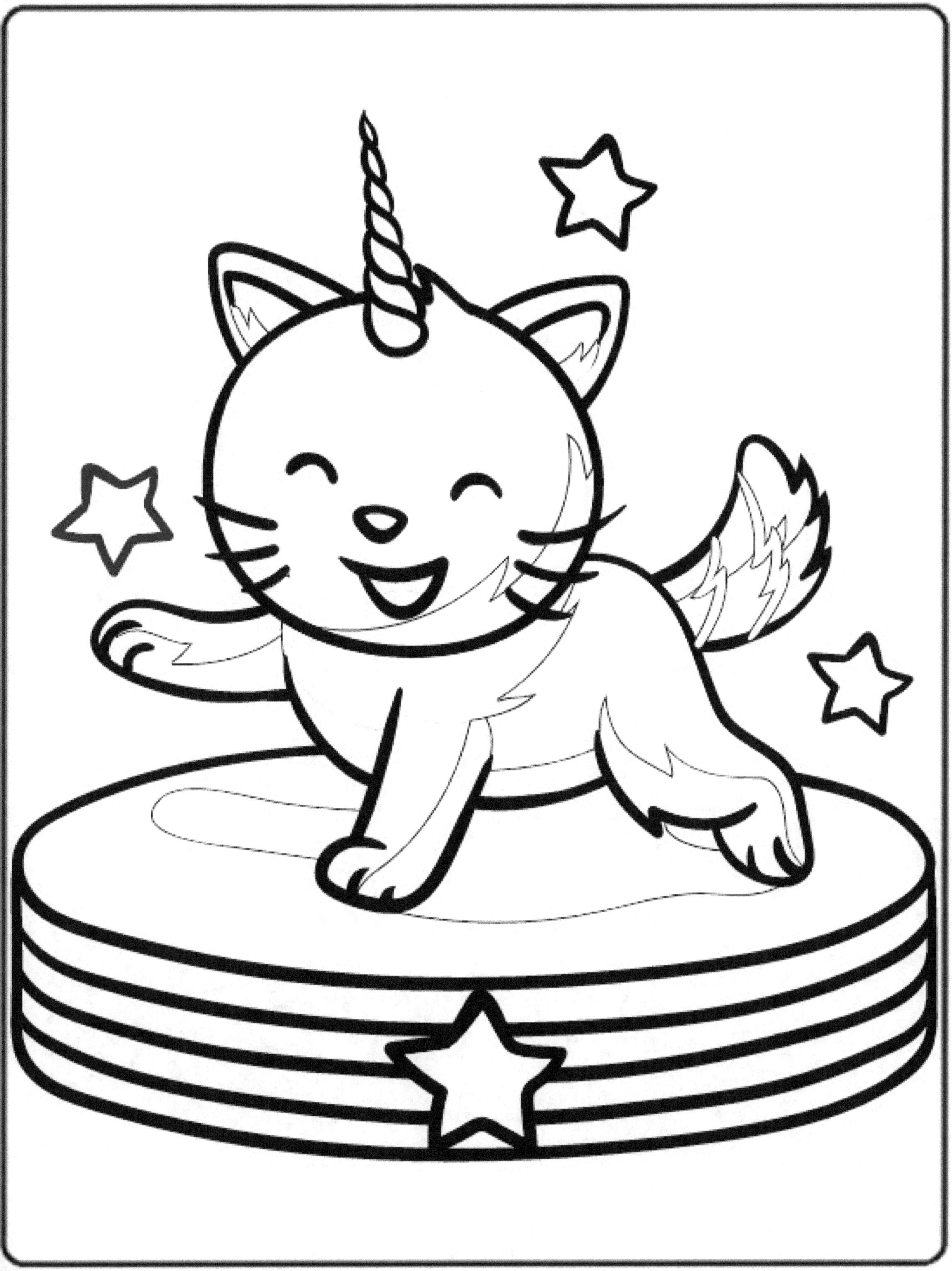

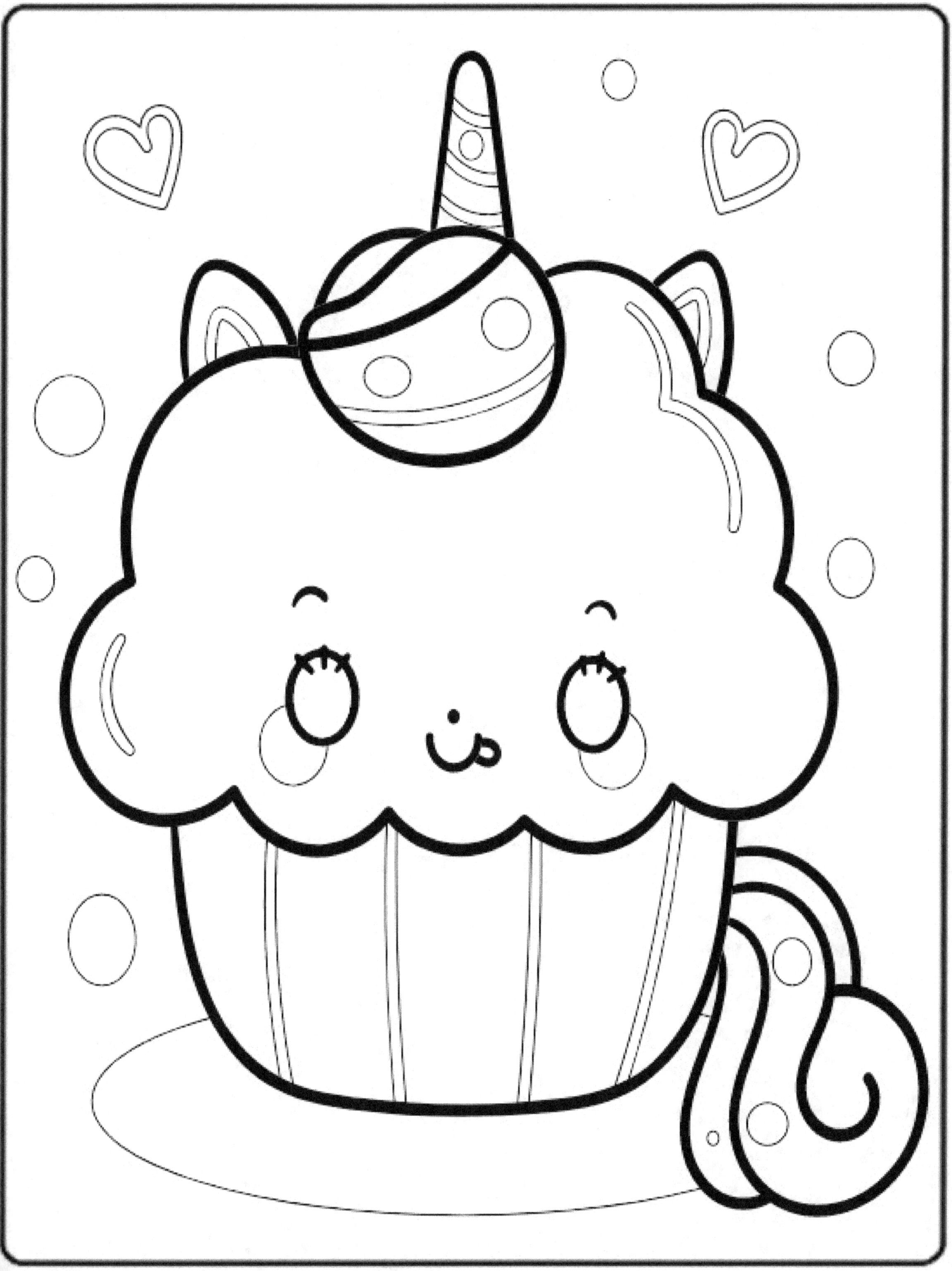

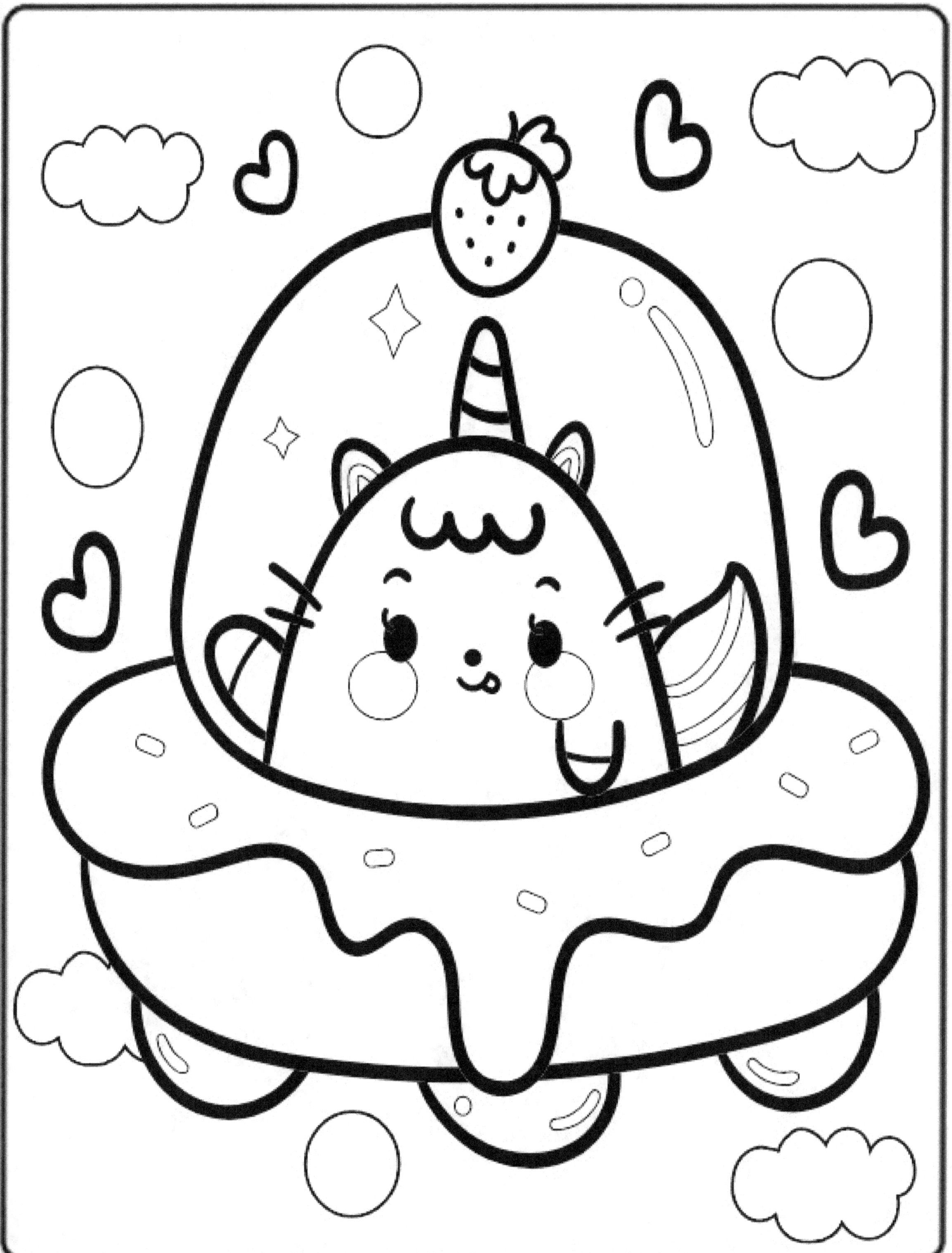

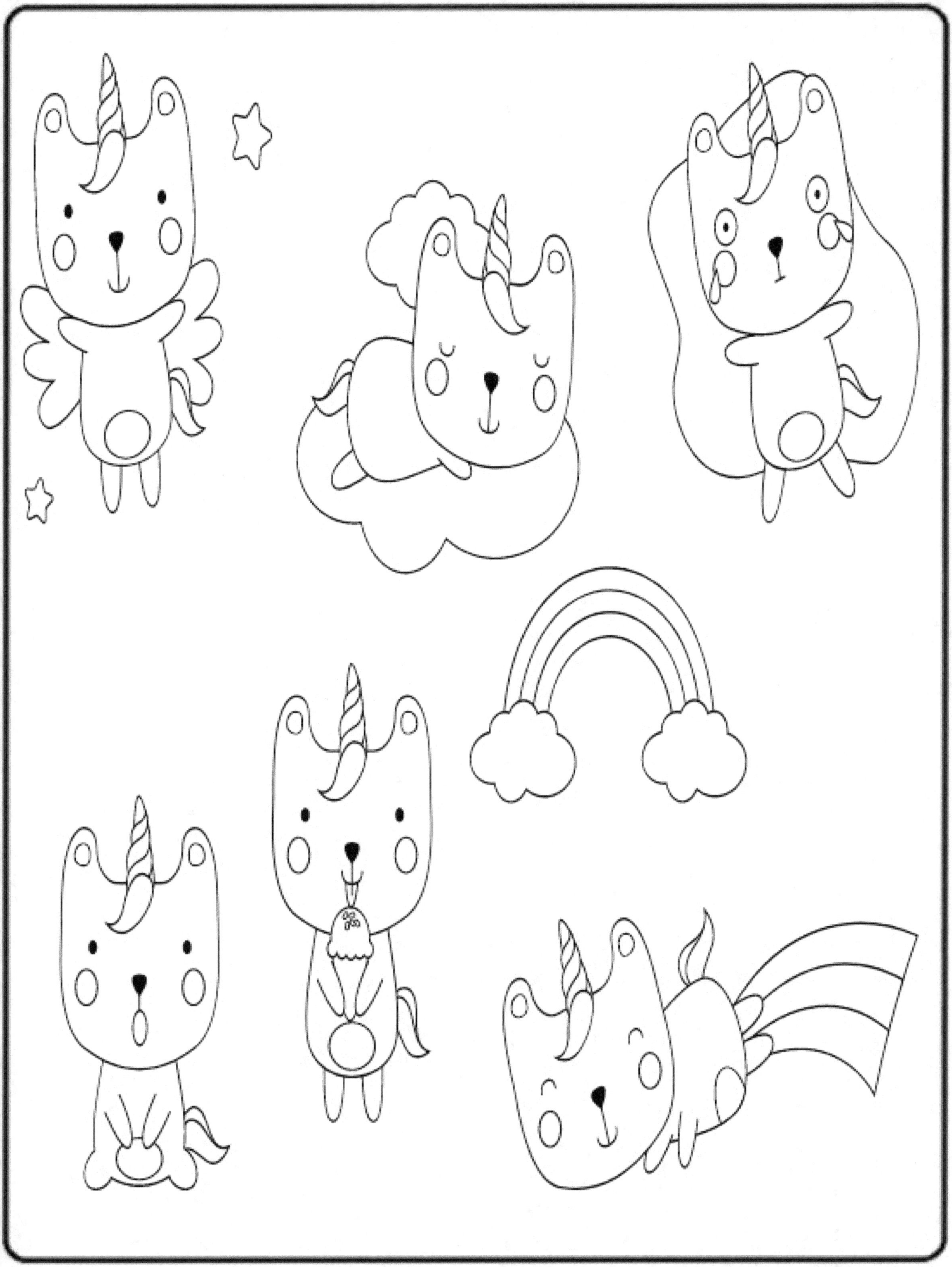

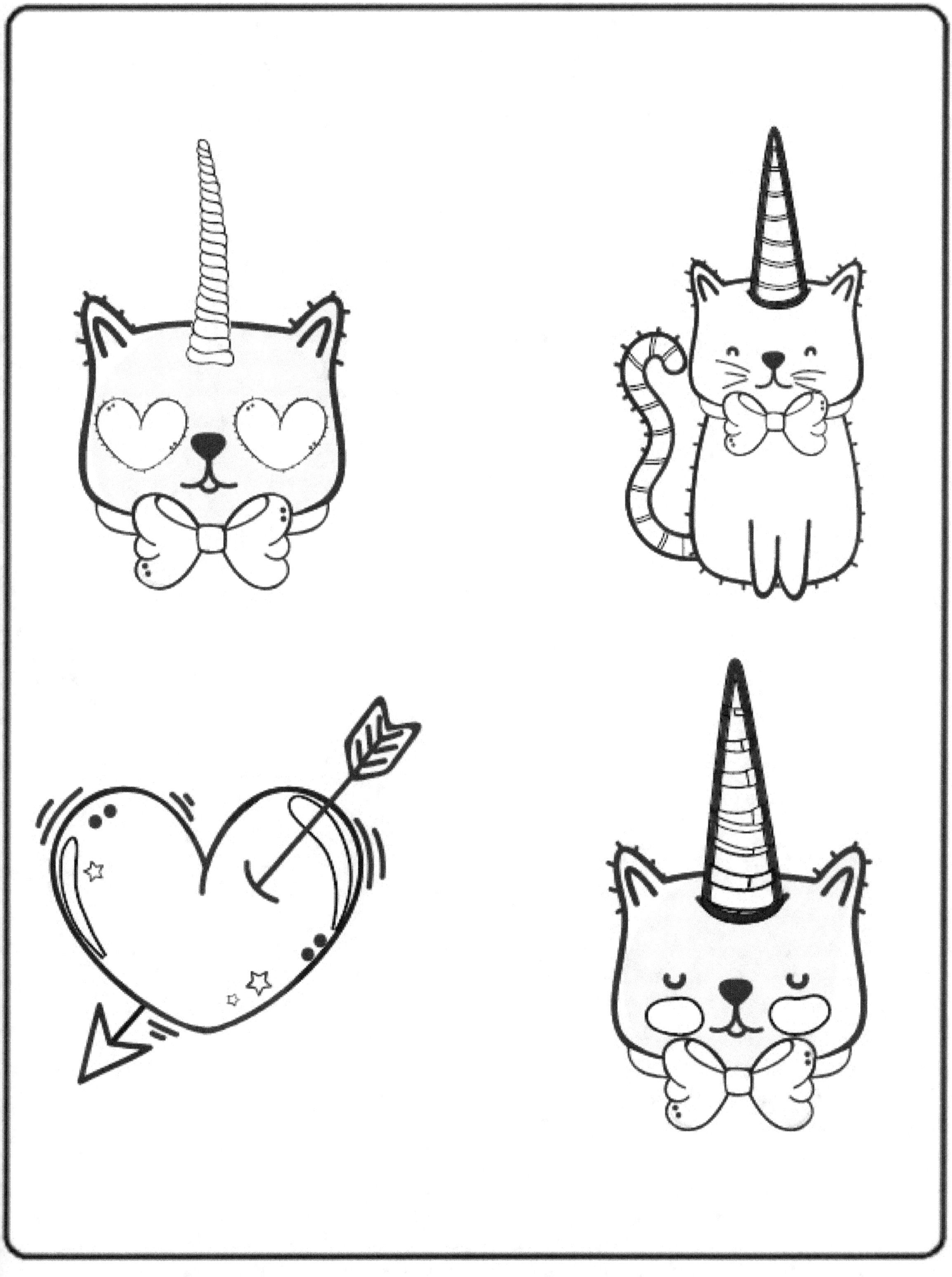

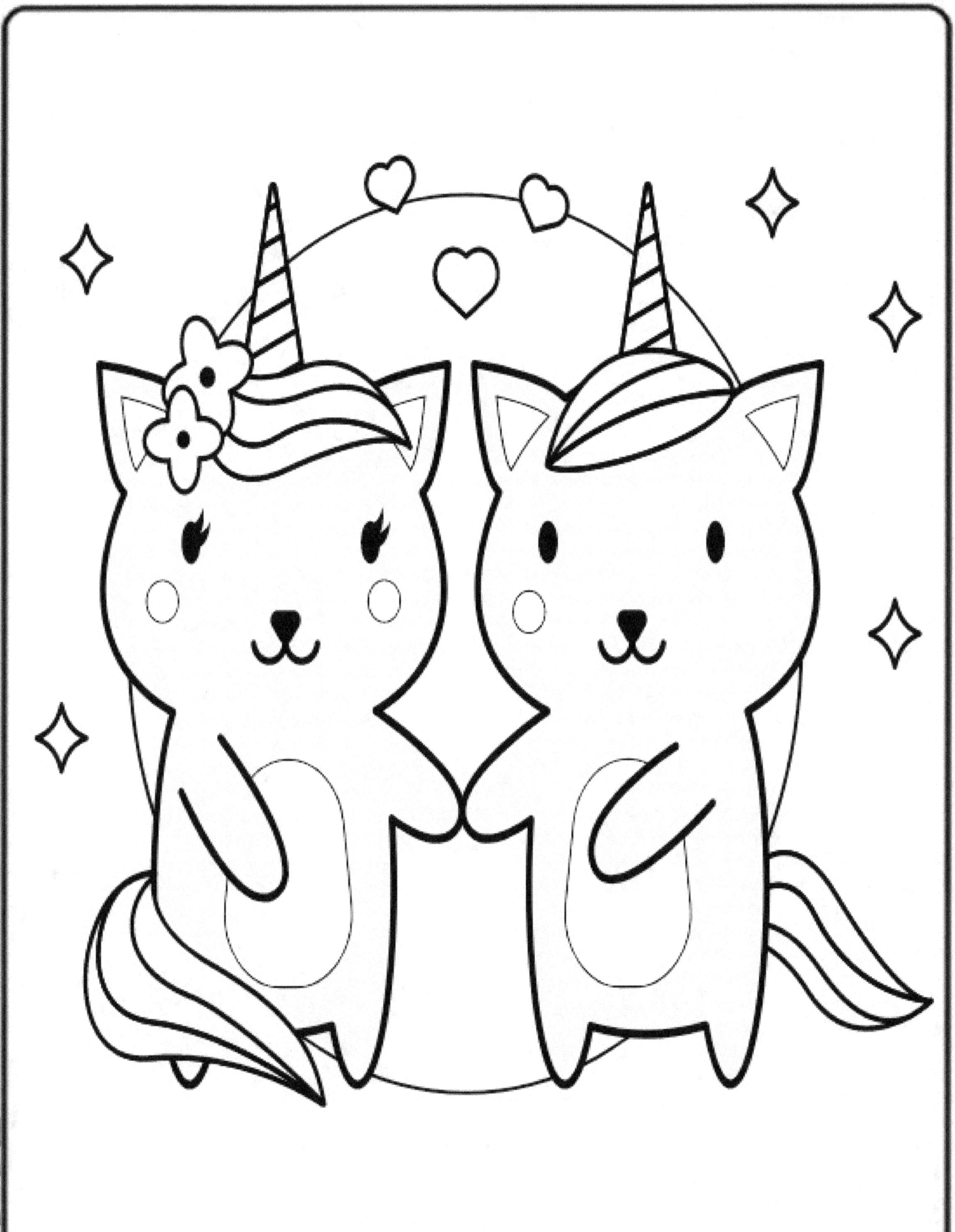

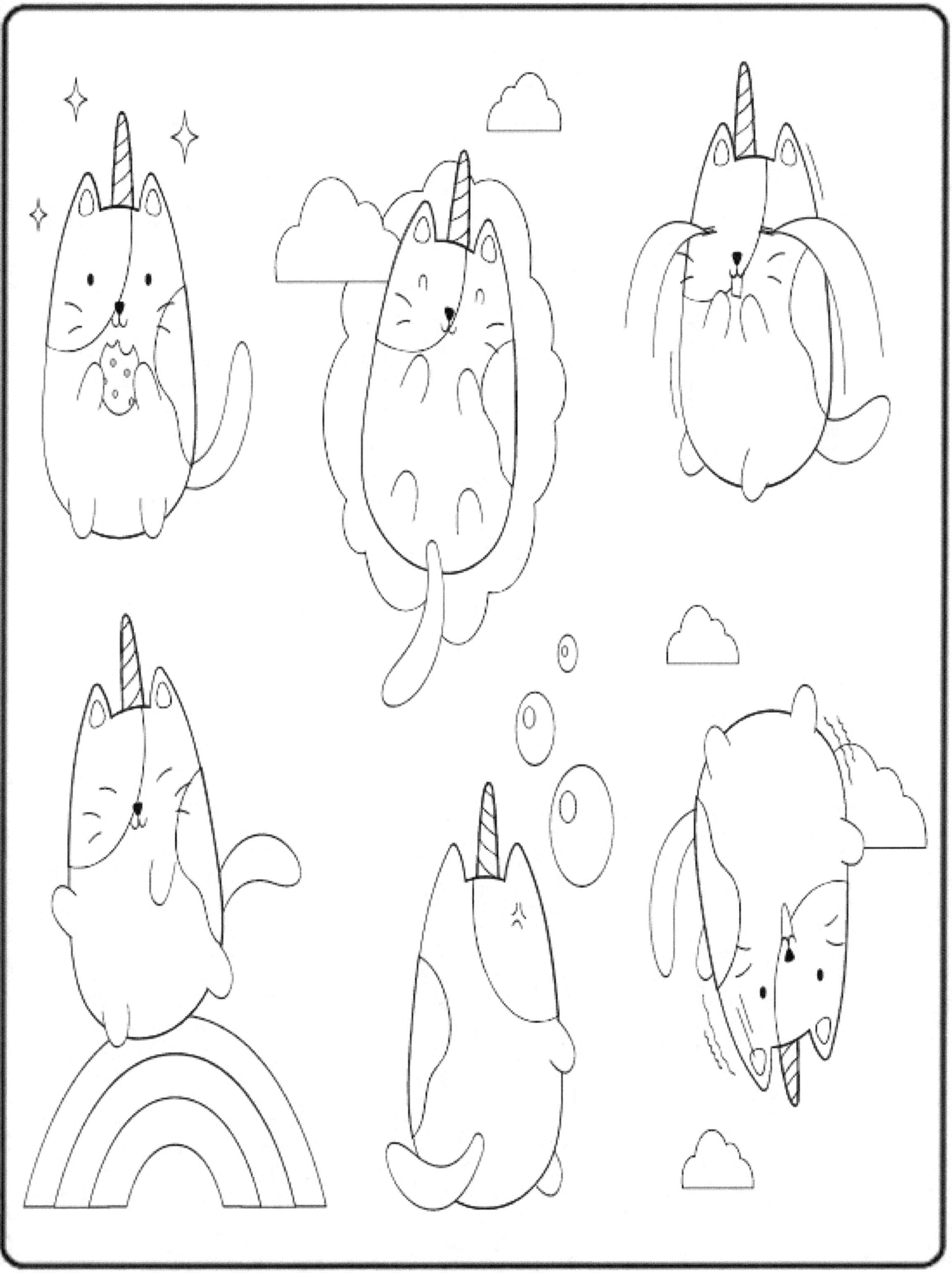

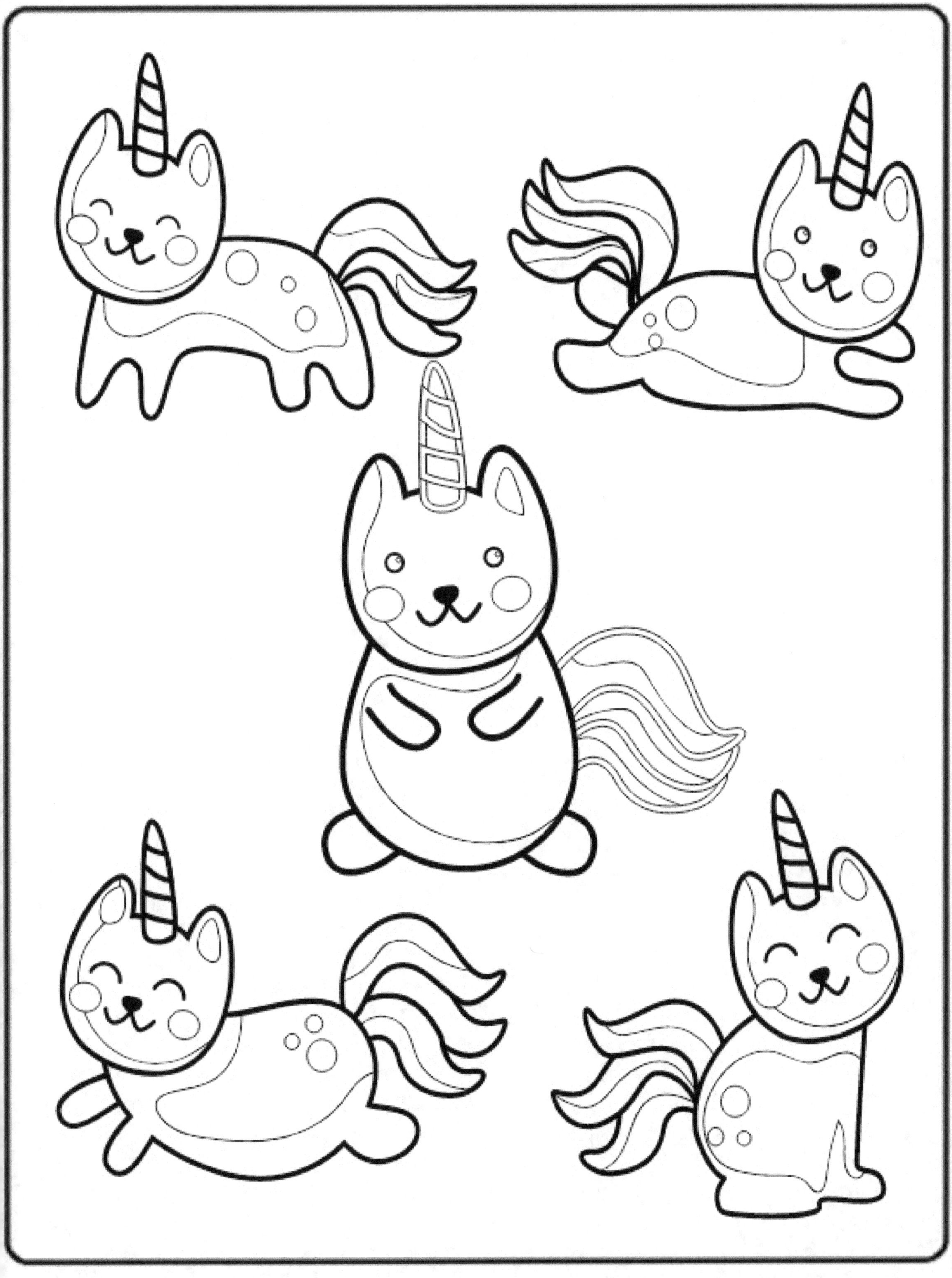

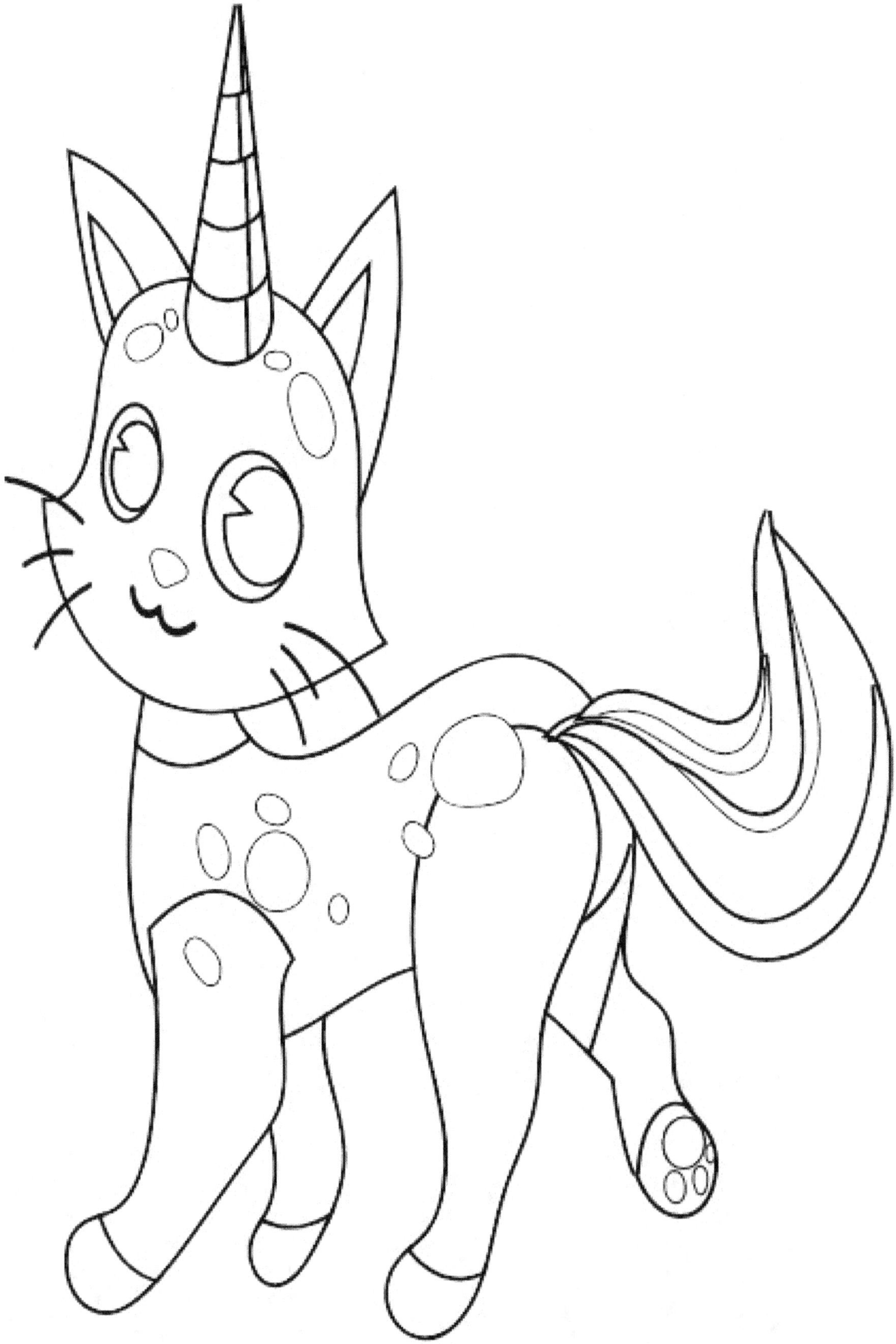

www.ingramcontent.com/pod-product-compliance
Lightning Source LLC
Chambersburg PA
CBHW080532220526
45465CB00006B/2683
* 9 7 9 8 6 5 7 3 6 6 8 6 0 *